COOL

Fashion

Street Style Coloring Book for Adult
Grownups and Girls

Adriana P. Jenova

Published by PUBLISHING COMPANY in 2016
First edition: First printing
Illustrations and design © 2016 Adriana P. Jenova

Author Contact
allcoloringbook.com

ISBN-13: 978-1533043597
ISBN-10: 1533043590

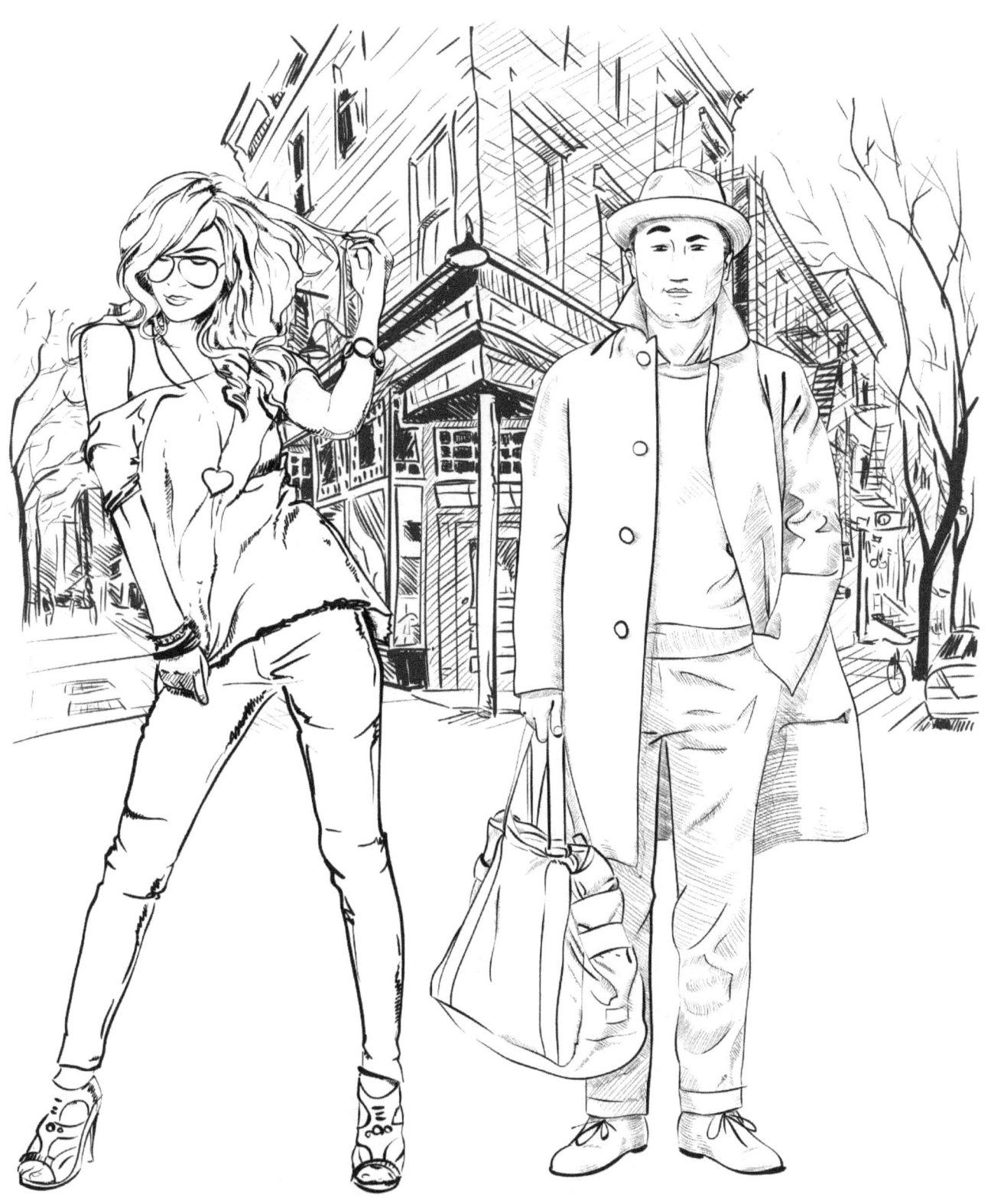

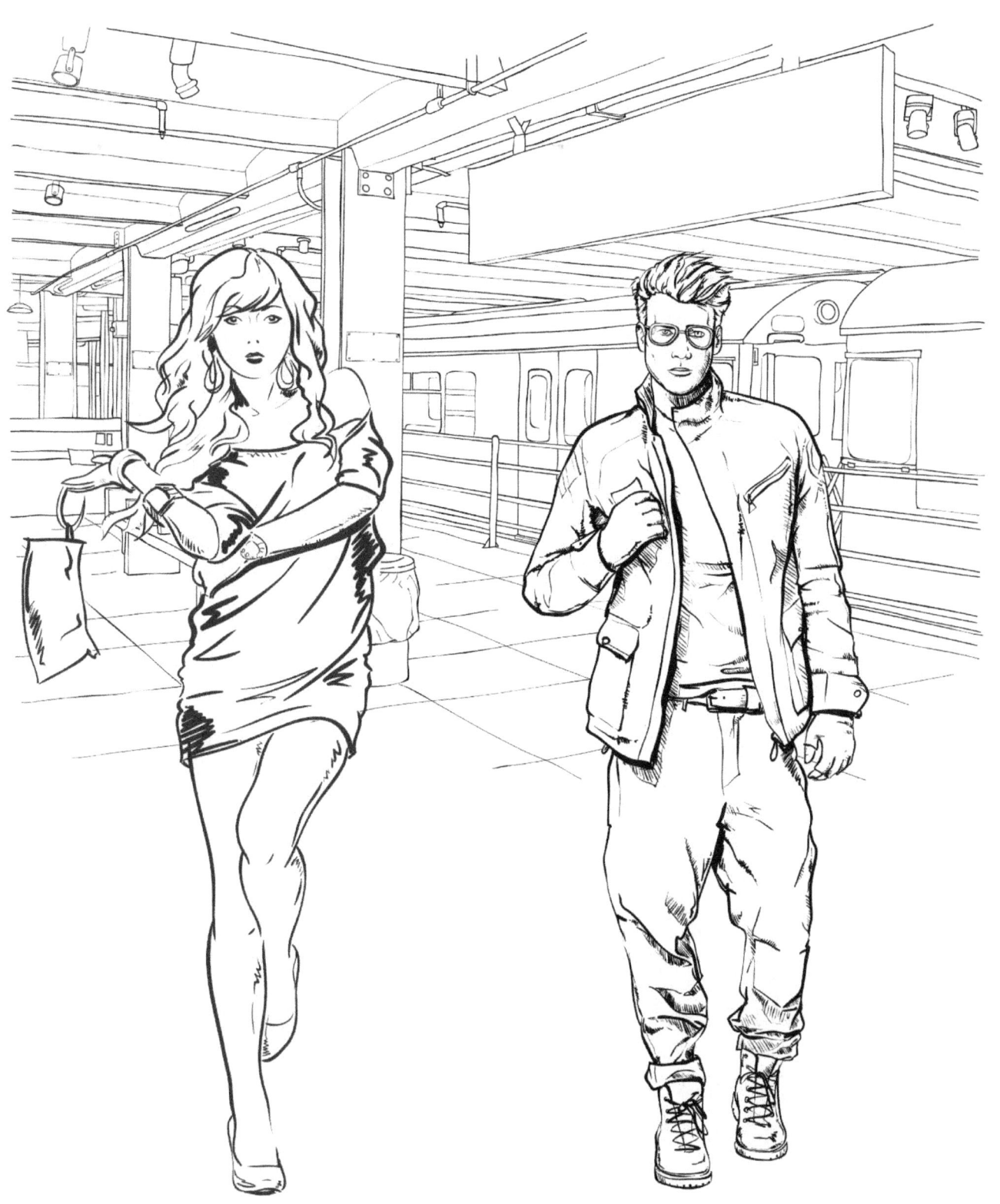

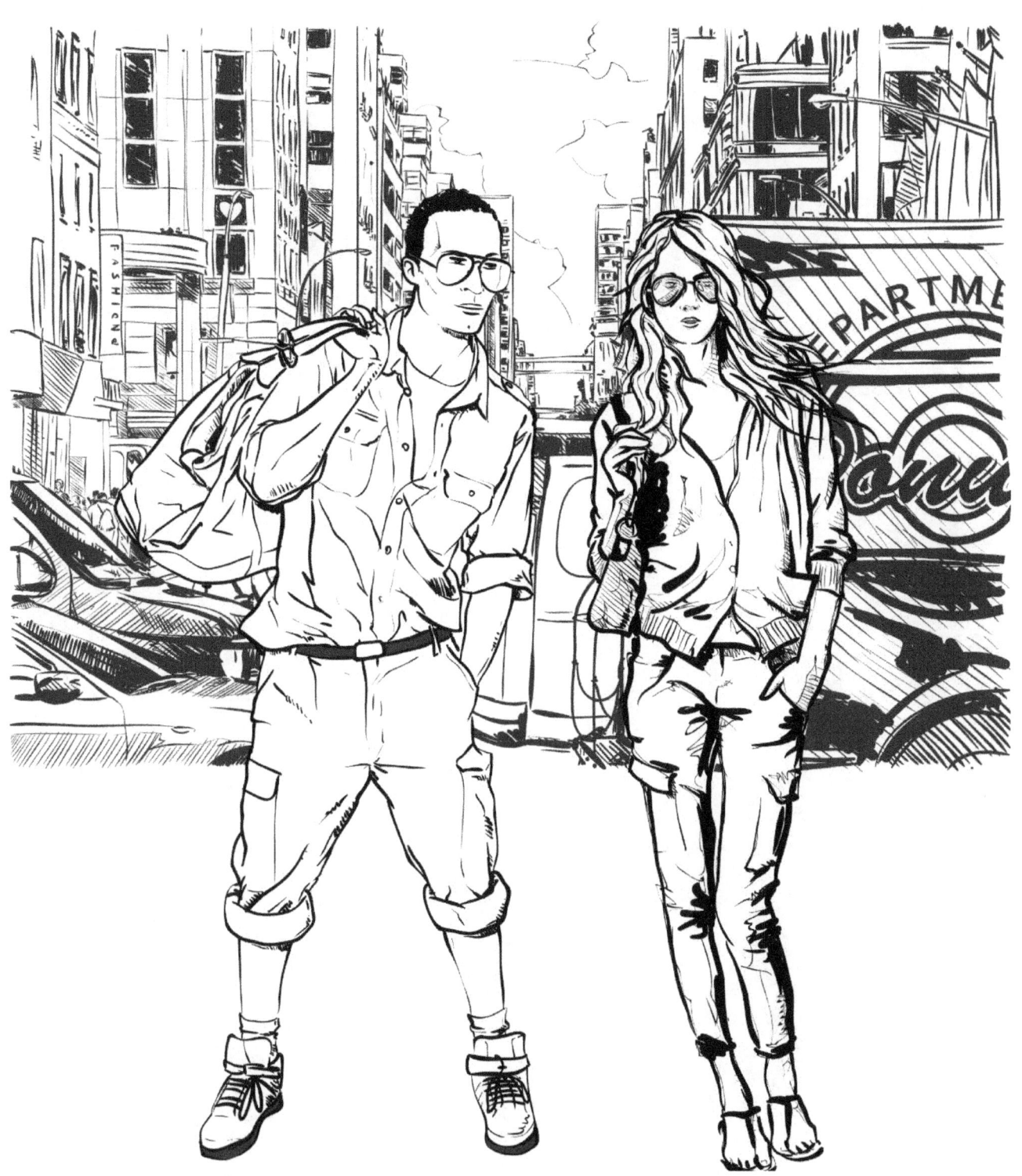

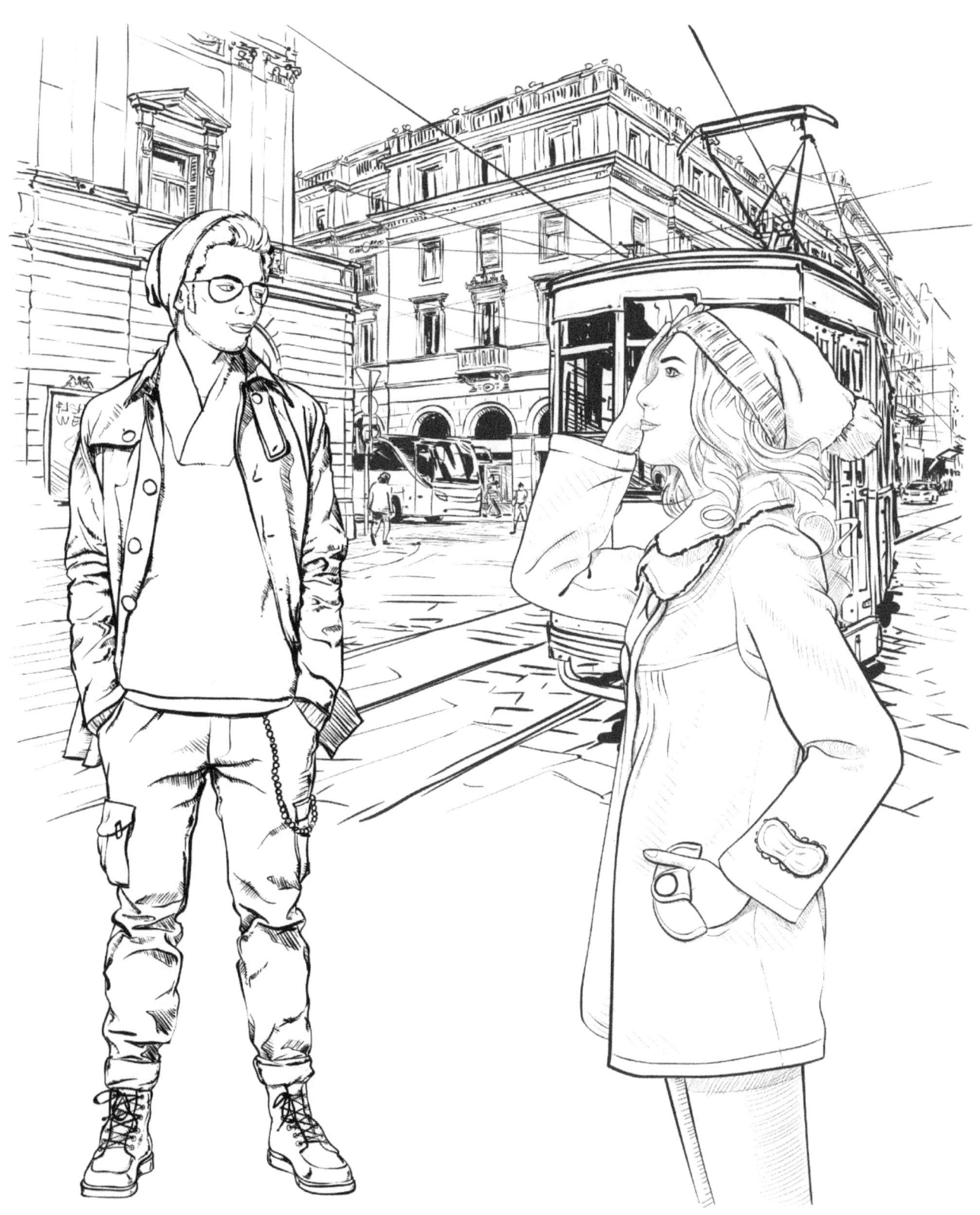

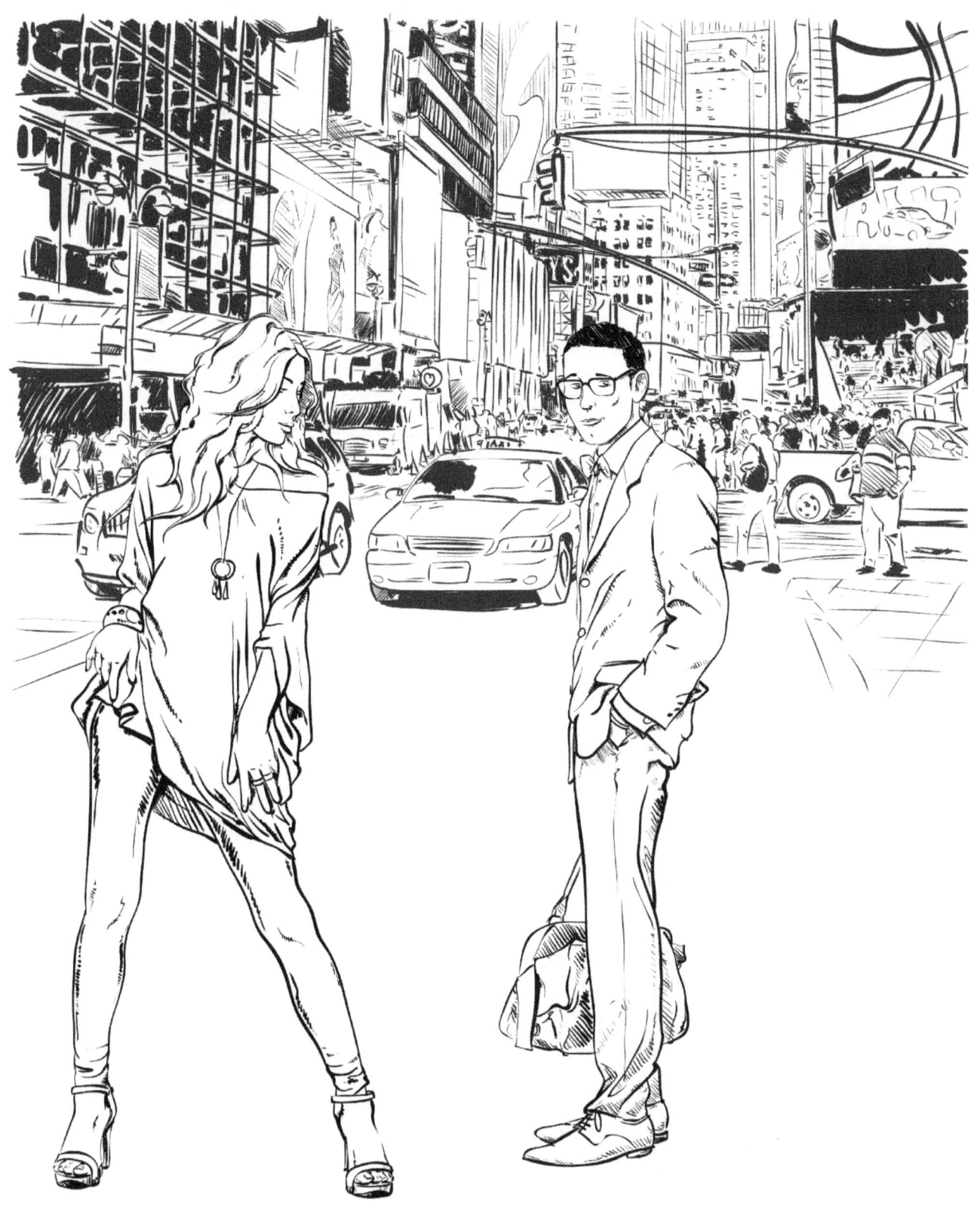

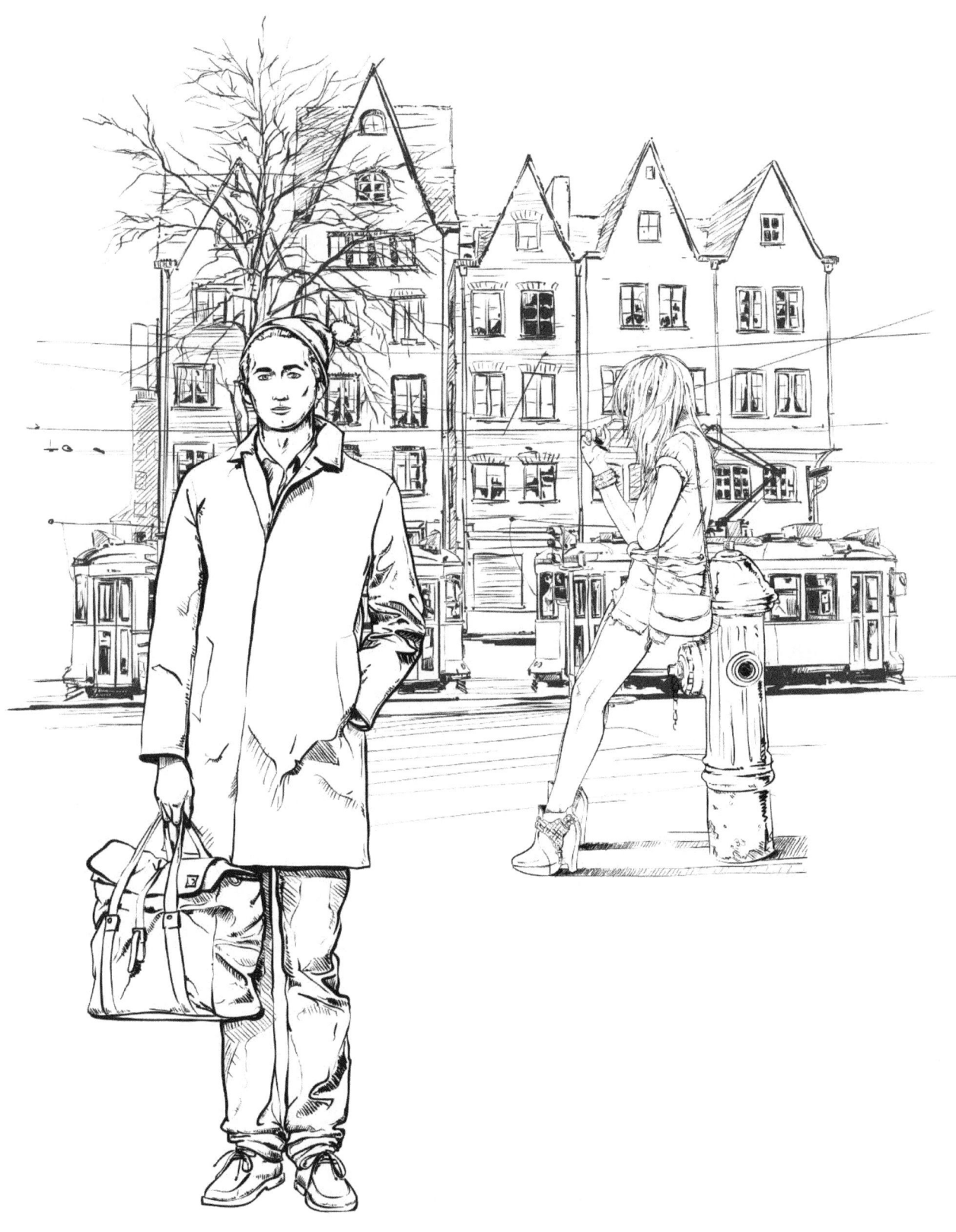

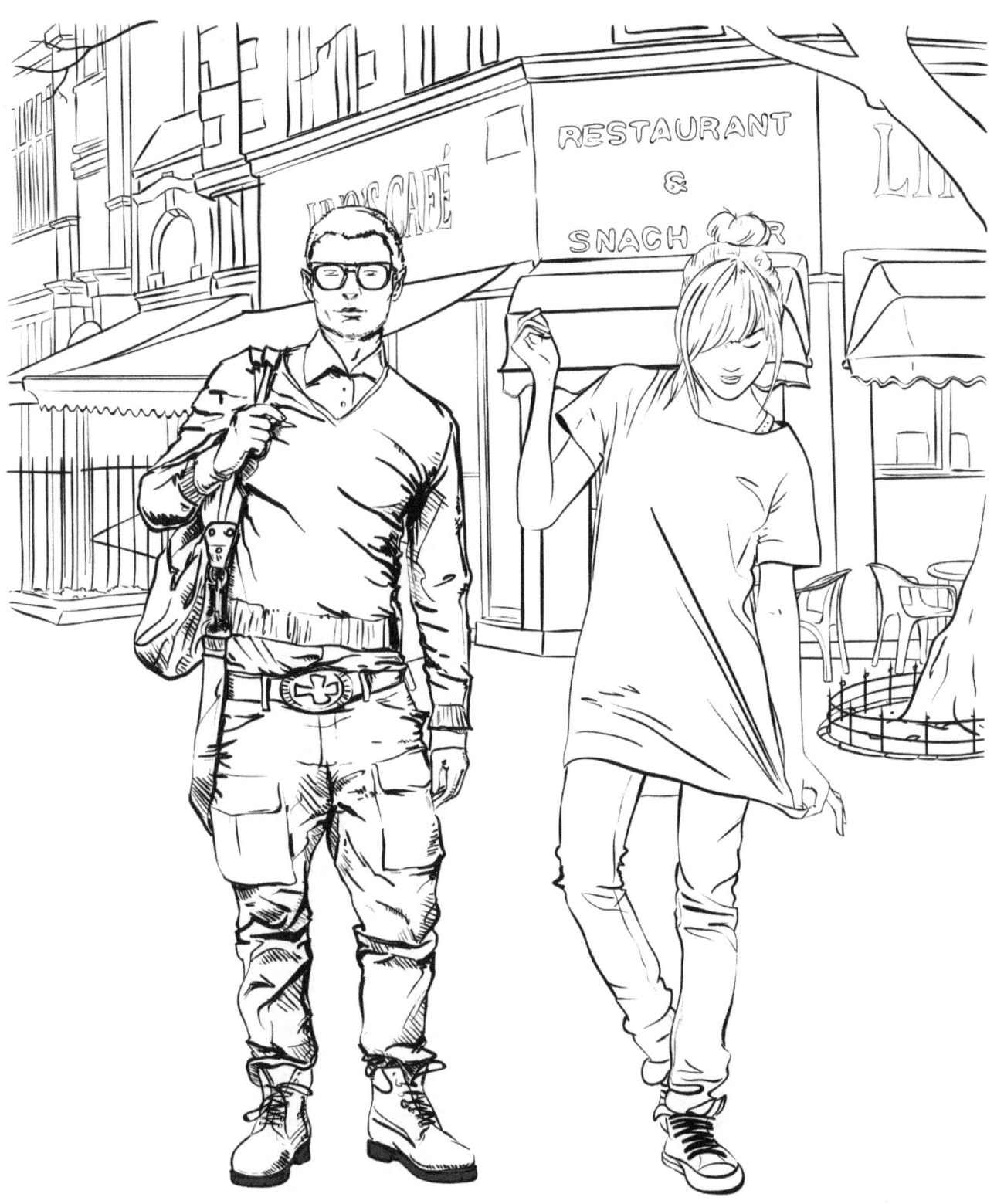

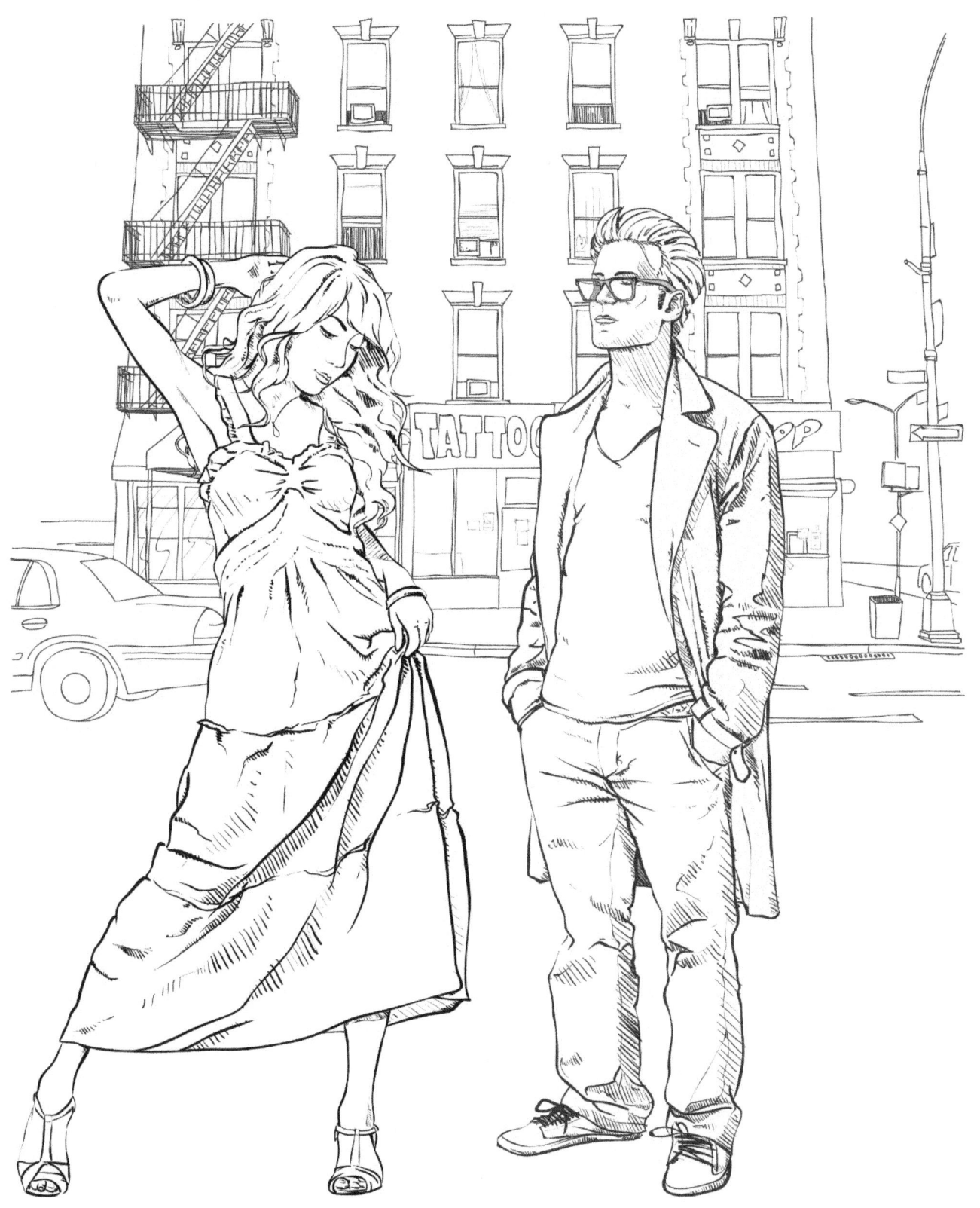

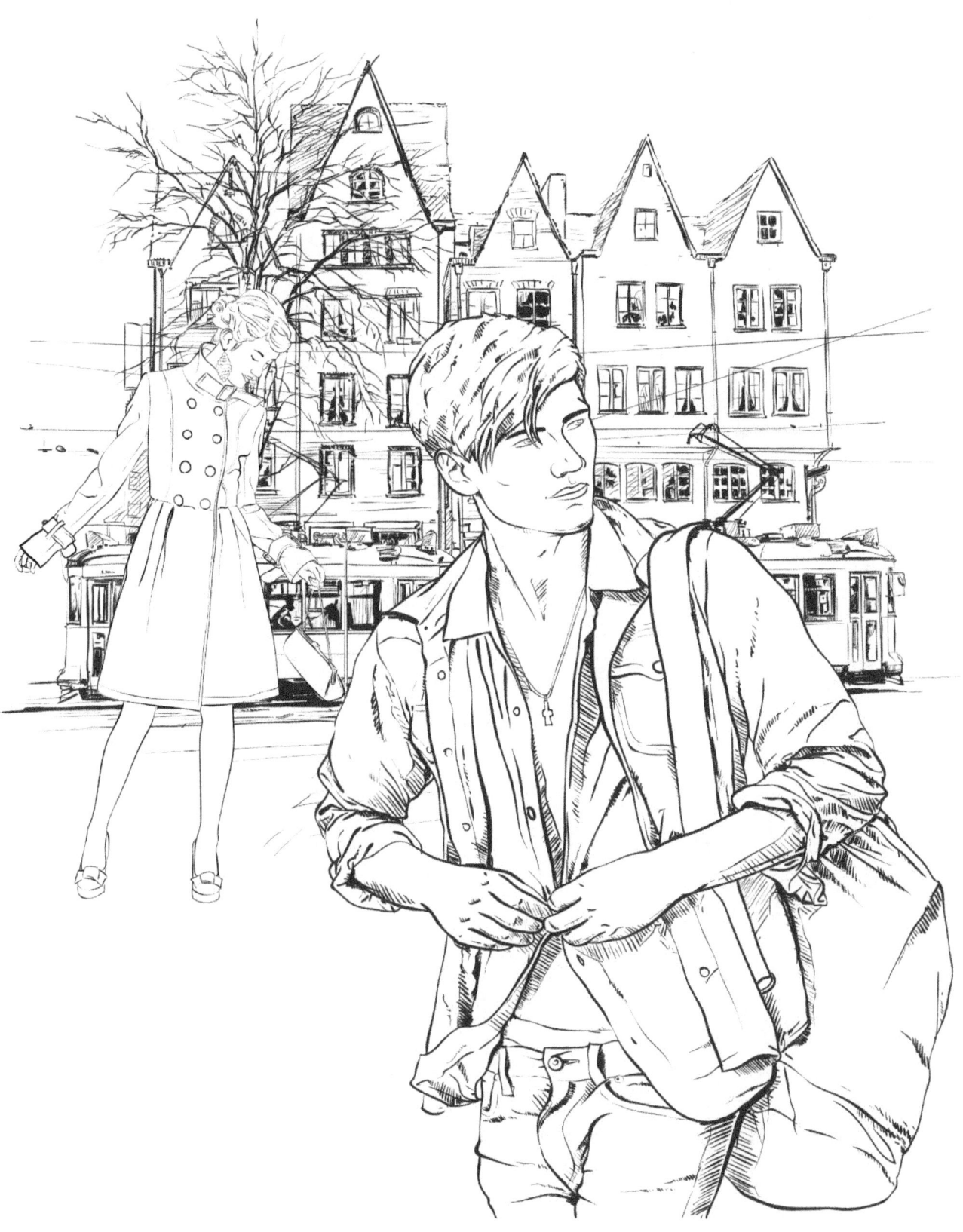

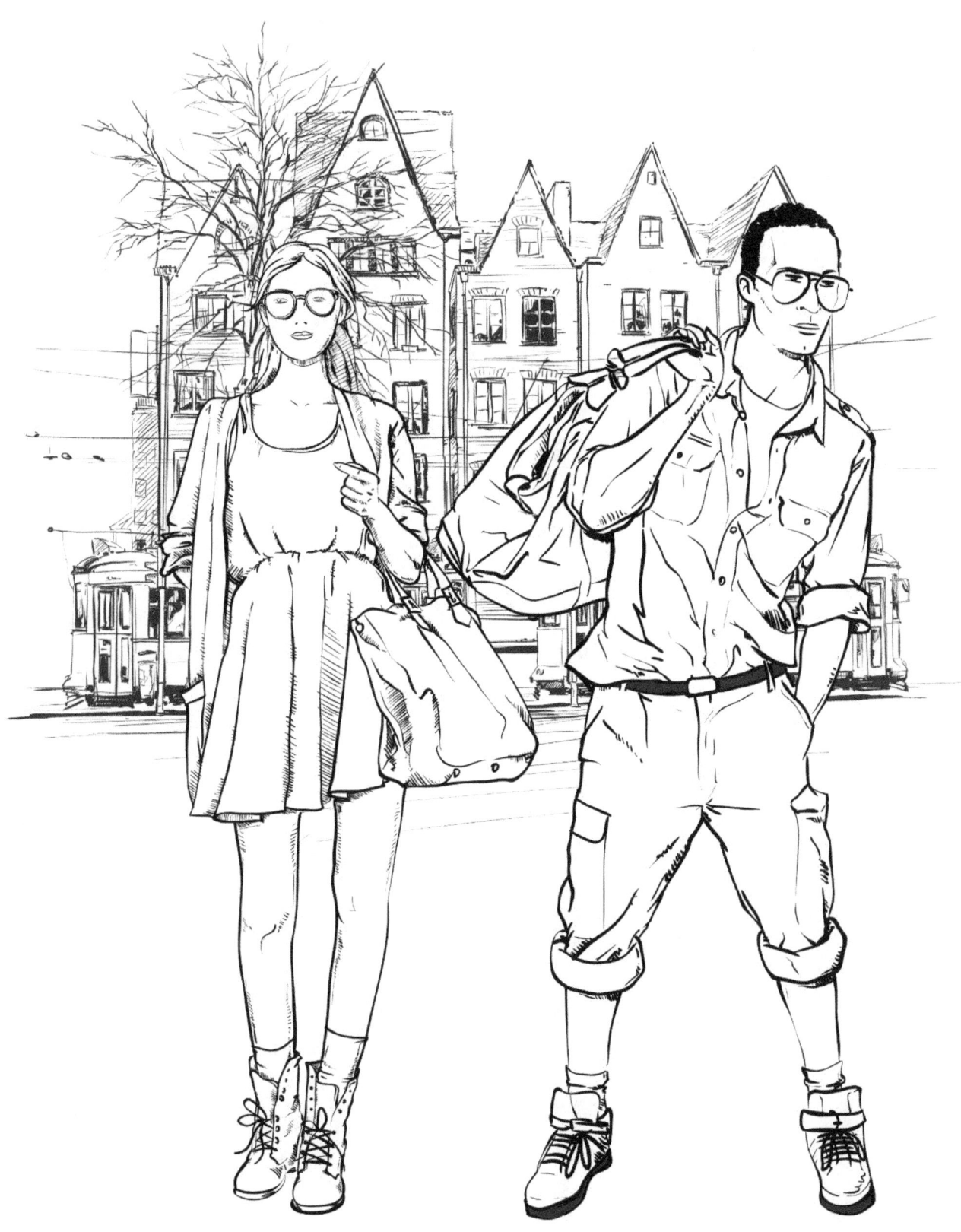

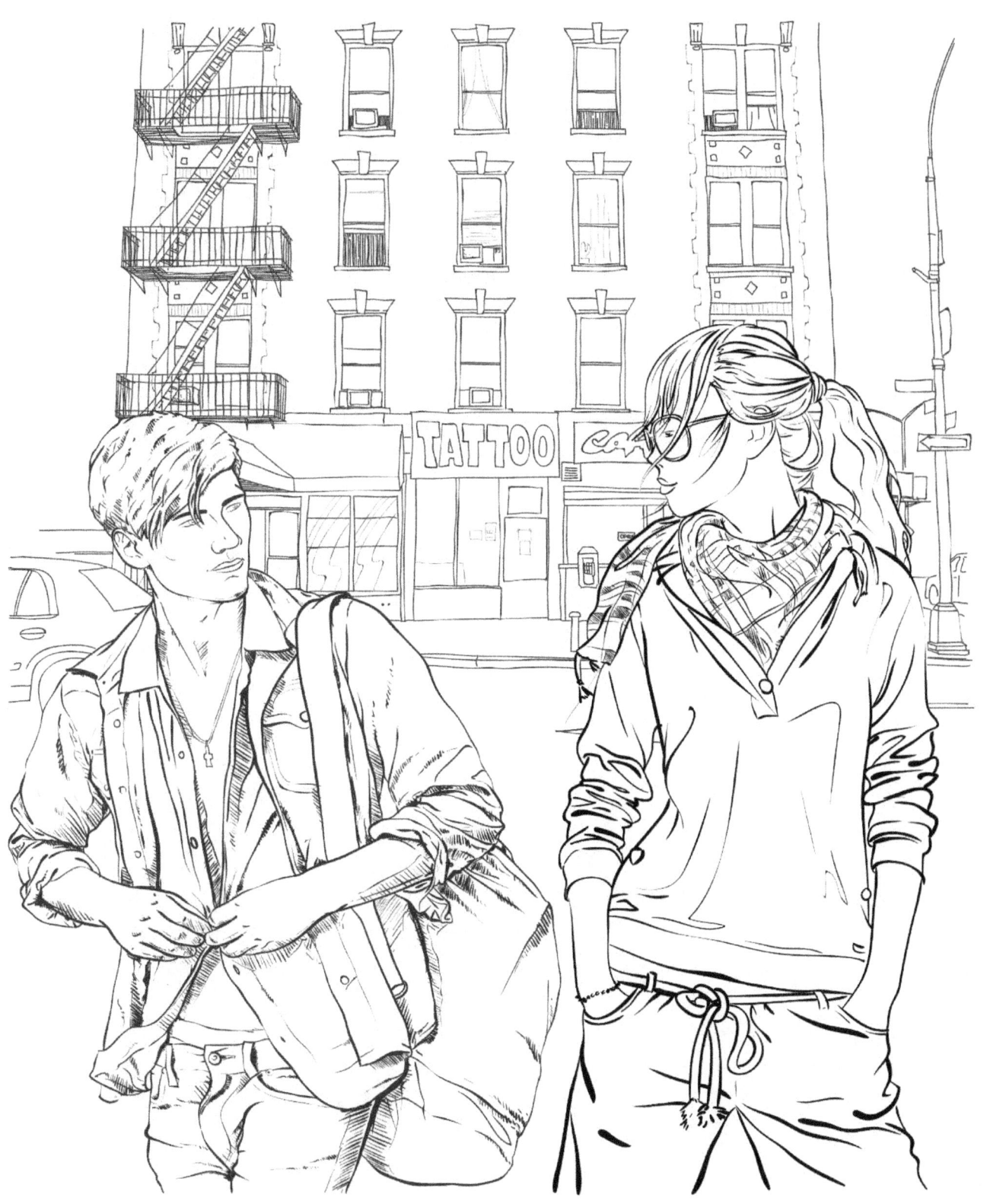

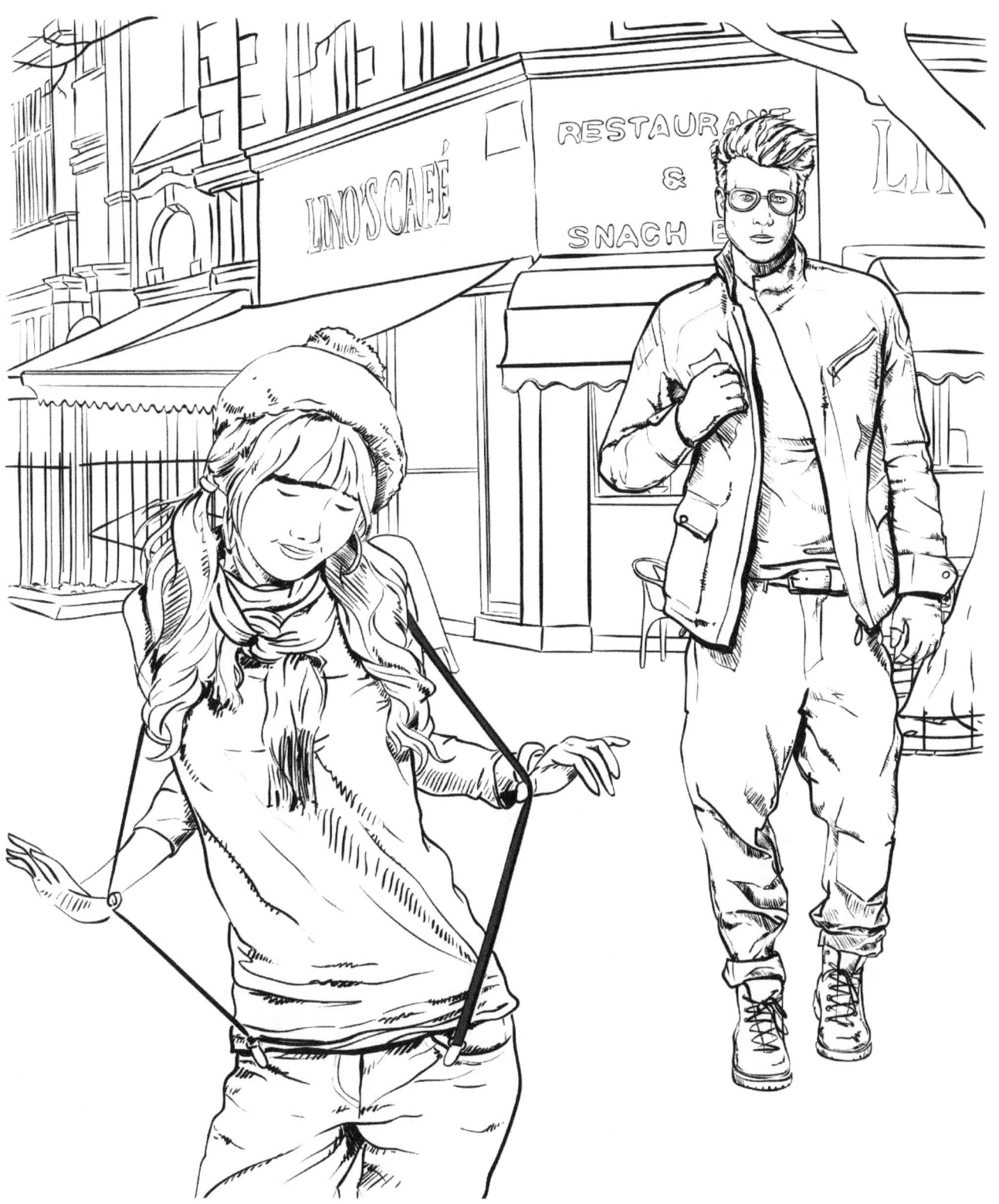

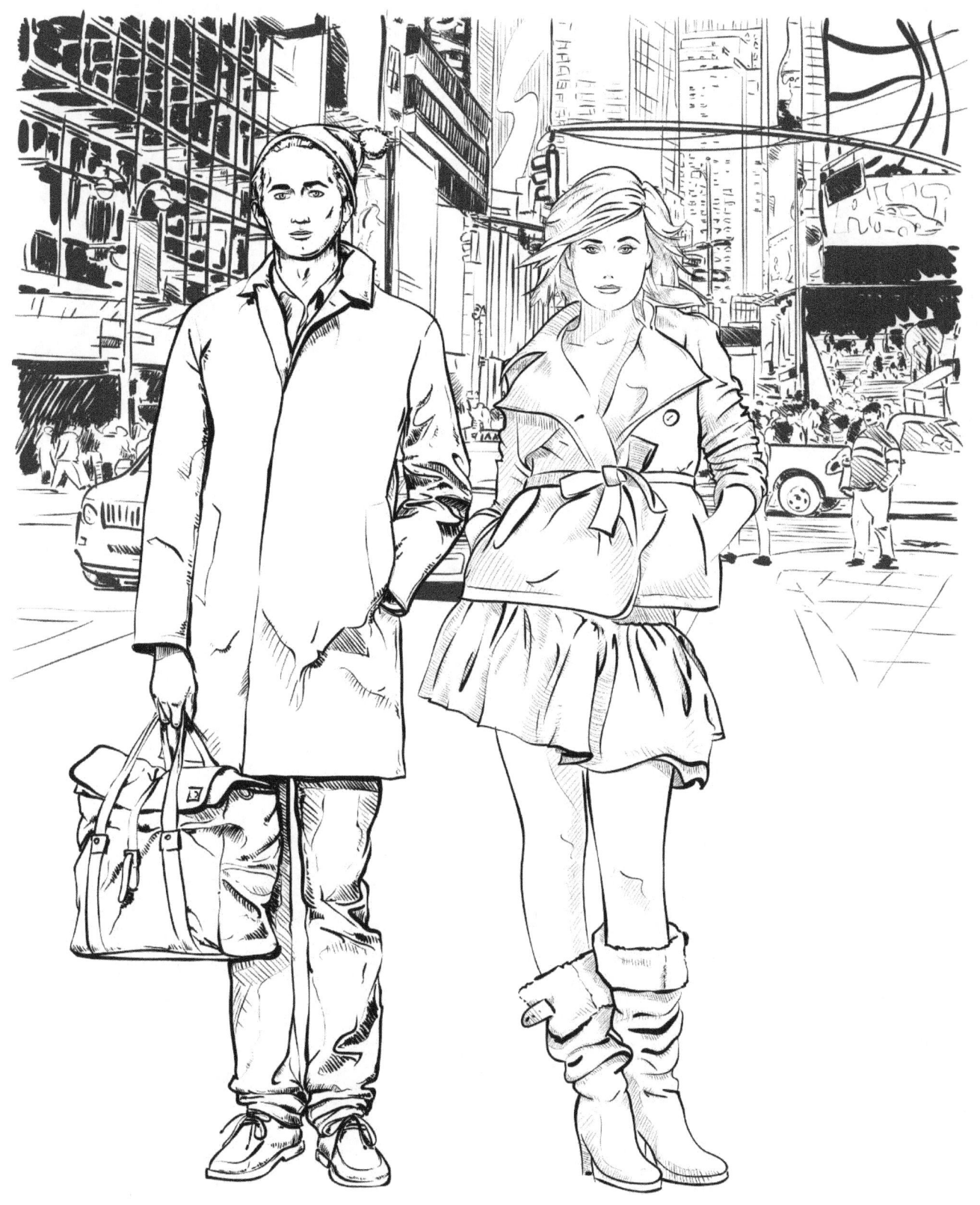

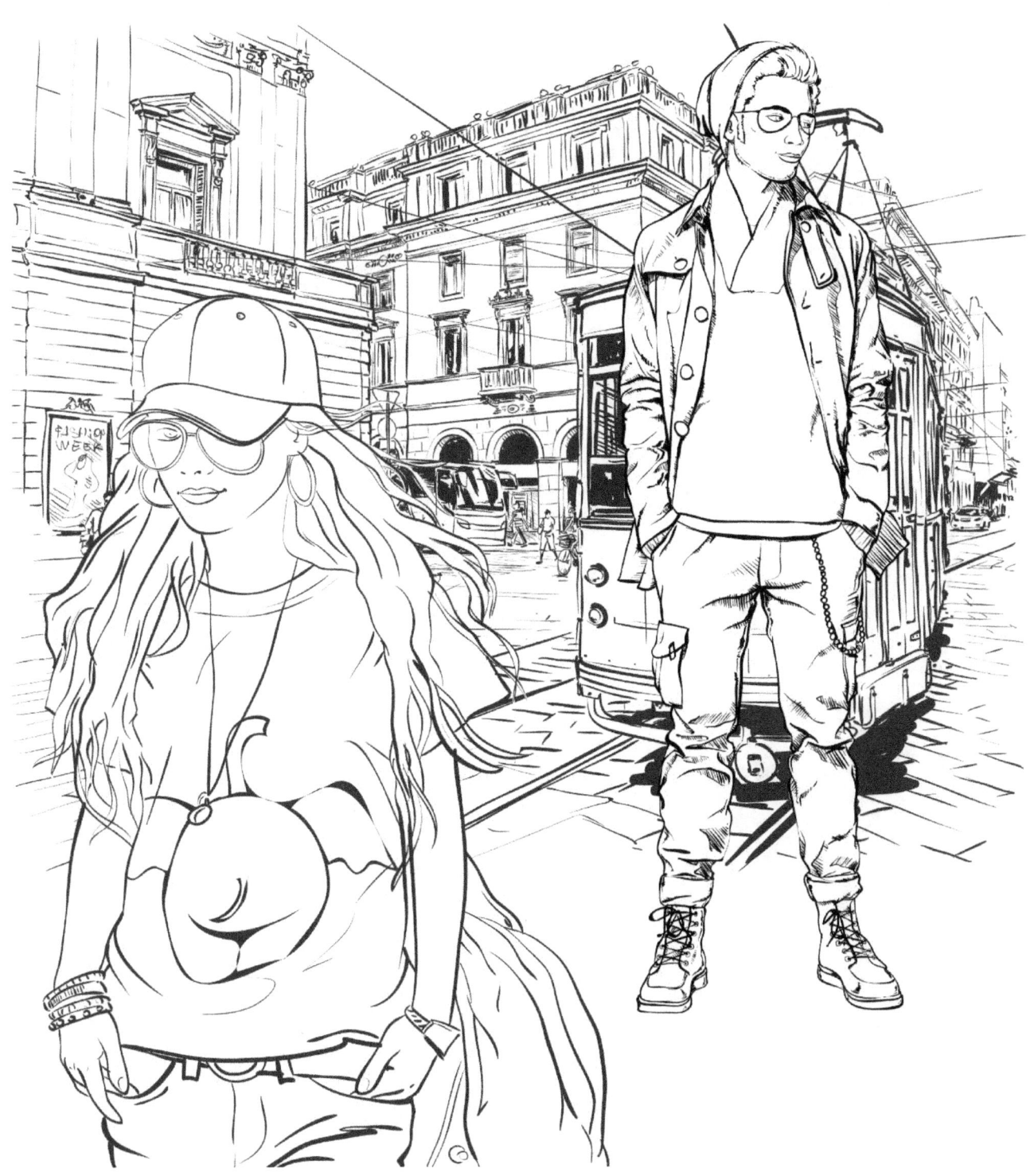

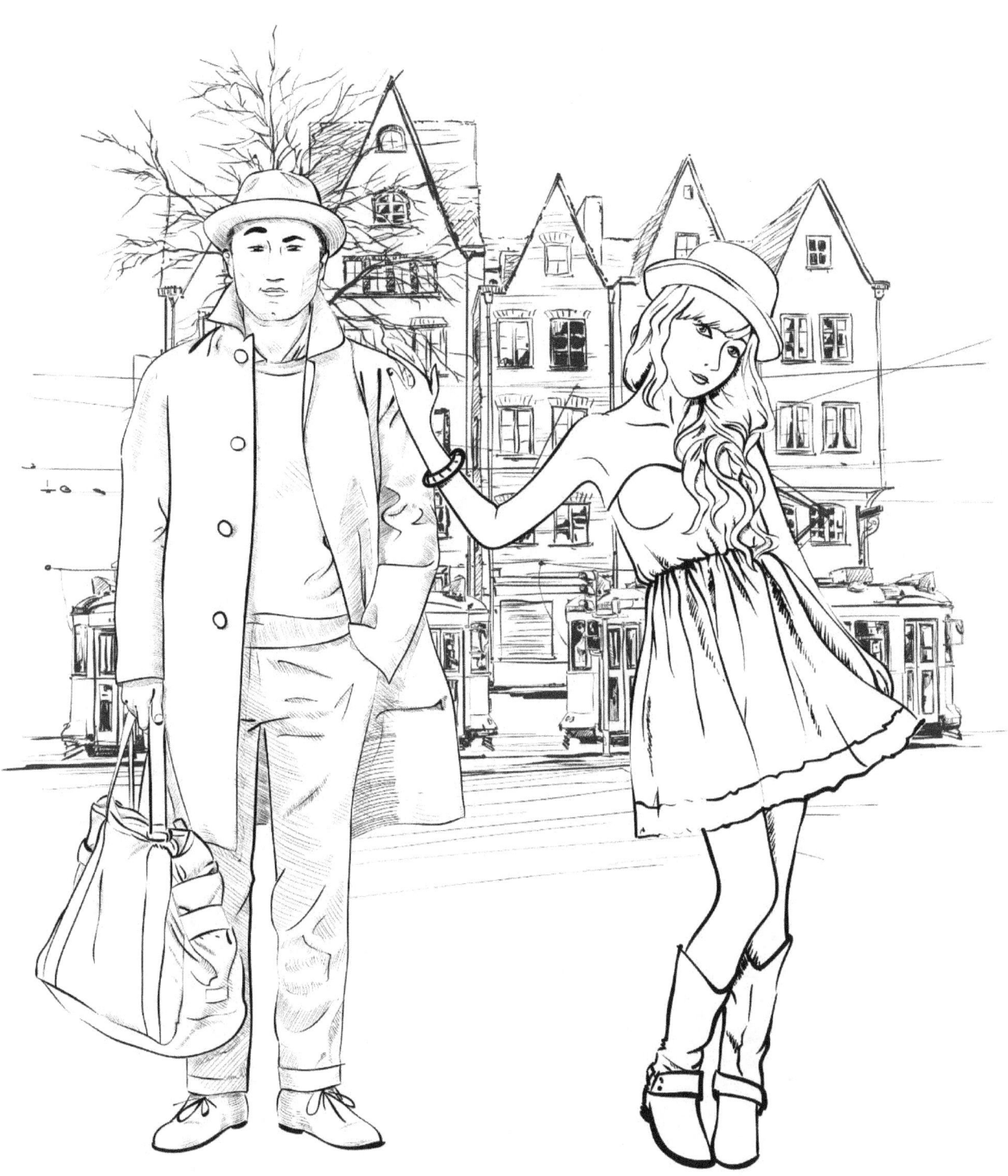

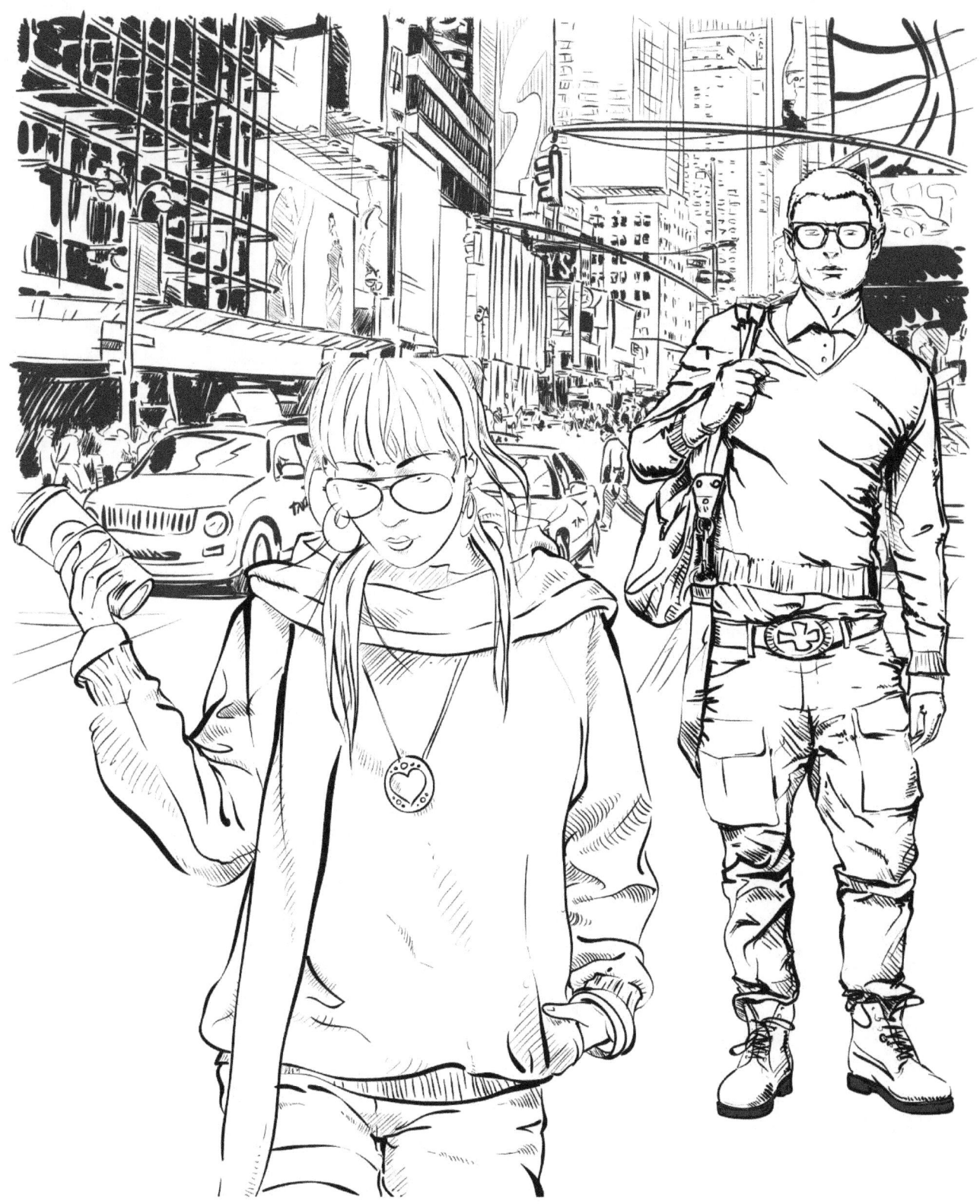

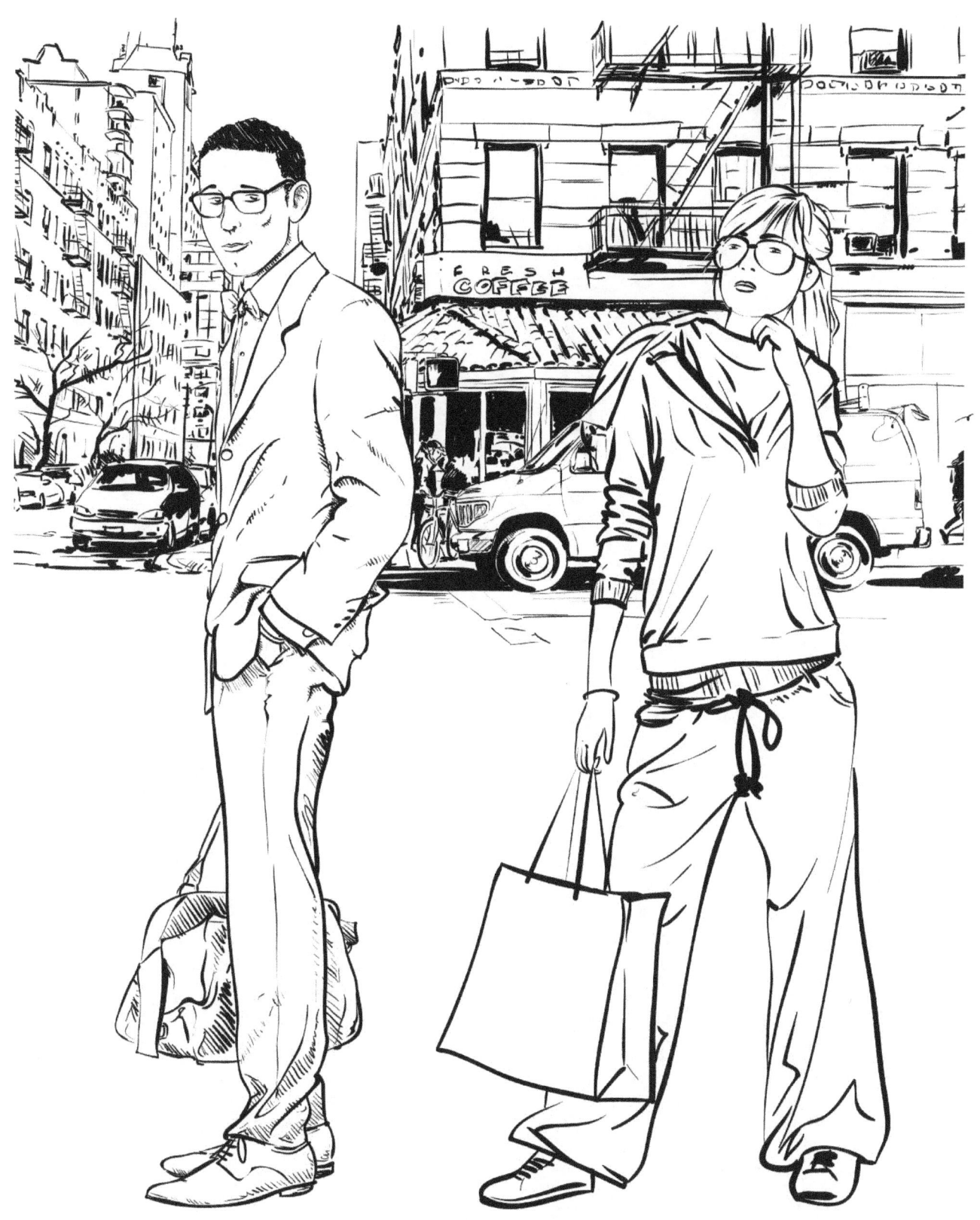

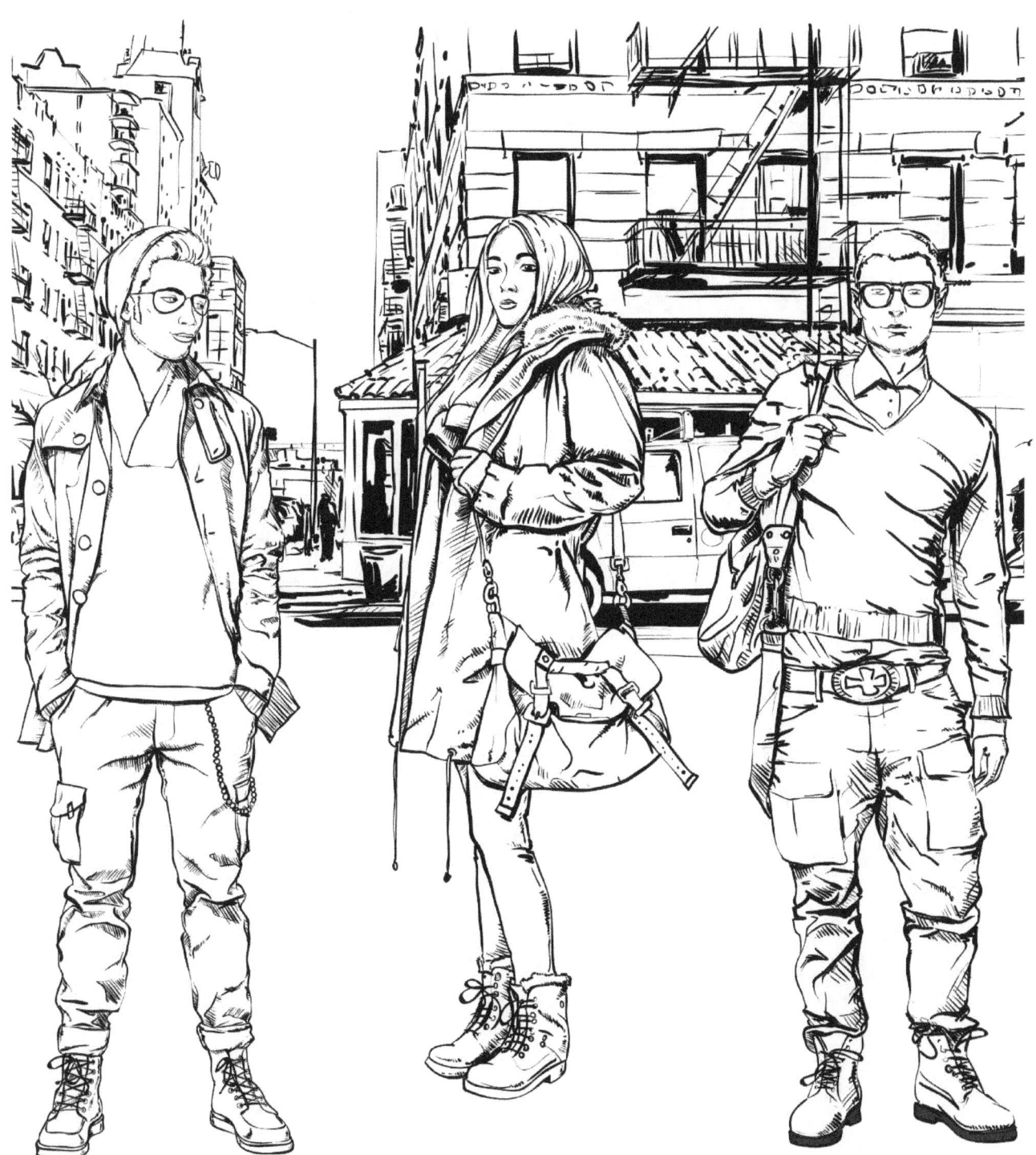

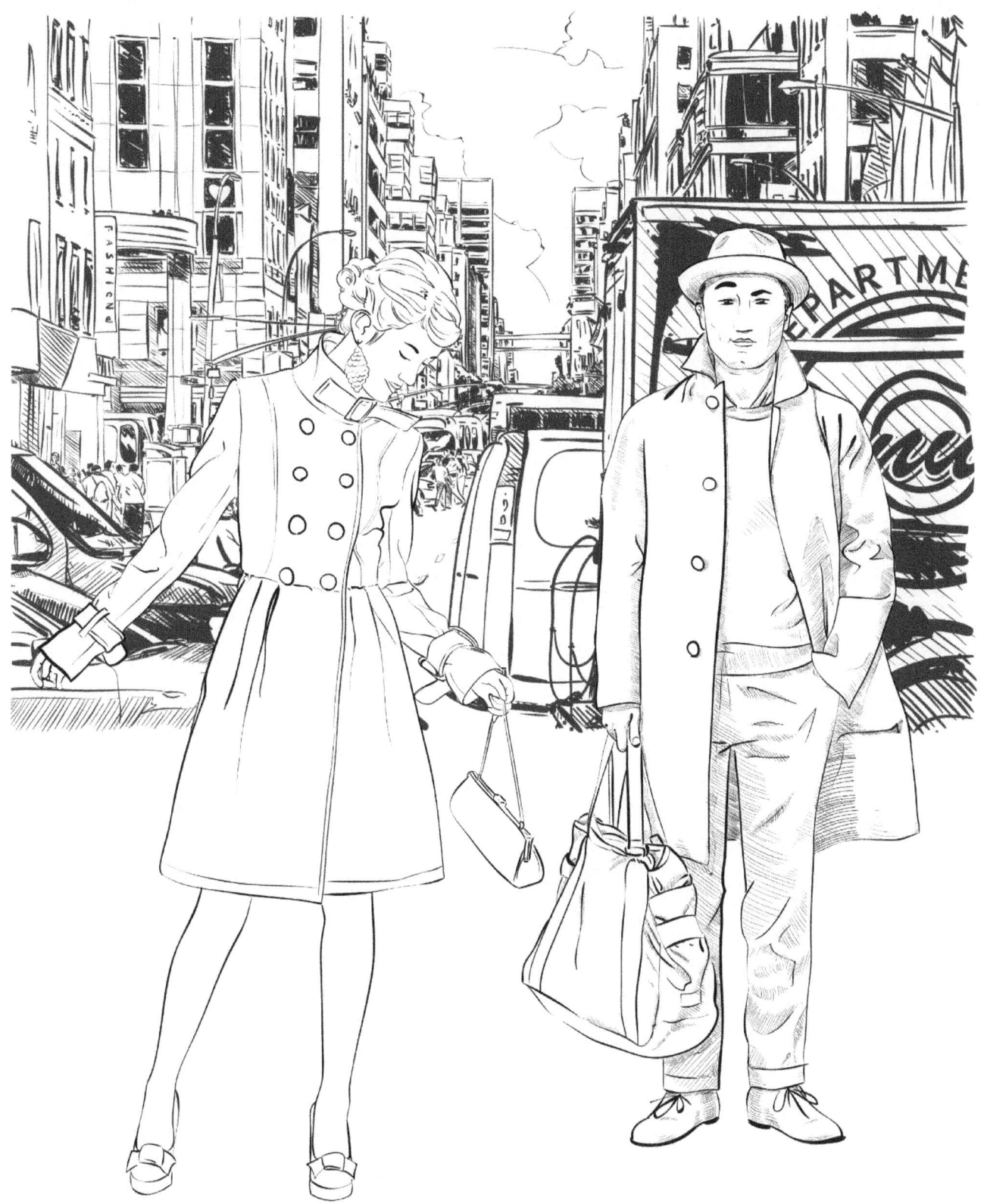

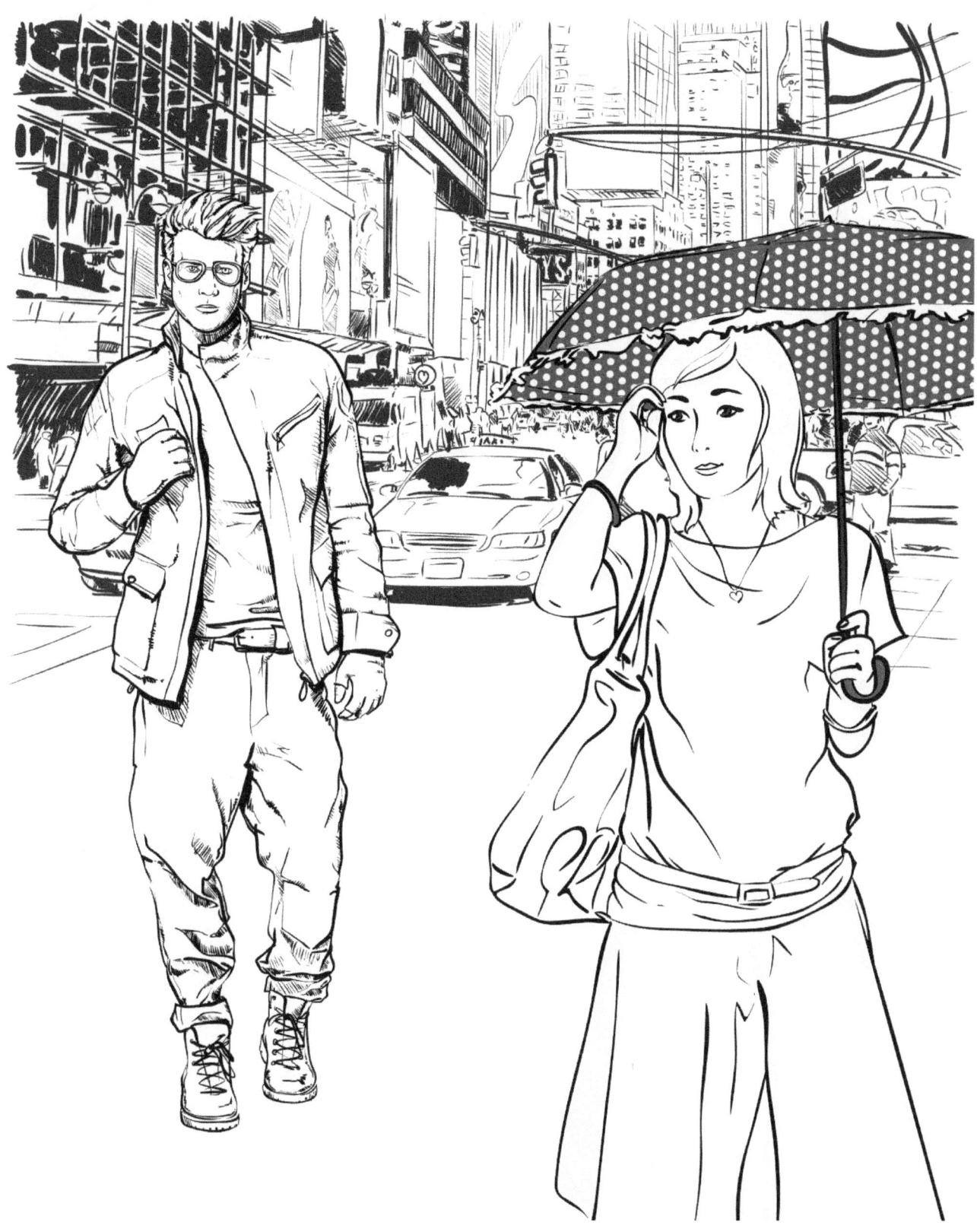

Thank You

Hope you've enjoyed your reading experience.

We here at Adriana P. Jenova will always strive to deliver to you the highest quality guides.

So I'd like to thank you for supporting us and reading until the very end.

Before you go, would you mind leaving us a review on Amazon?

It will mean a lot to us and support us creating high quality guides for you in the future.

Thanks once again and here's where you can leave a review.

Get Free Ebook Coloring Page below

www.allcoloringbook.com

Warmly yours,
Adriana P. Jenova Team

www.ingramcontent.com/pod-product-compliance
Lightning Source LLC
Chambersburg PA
CBHW080643190526
45169CB00009B/3475